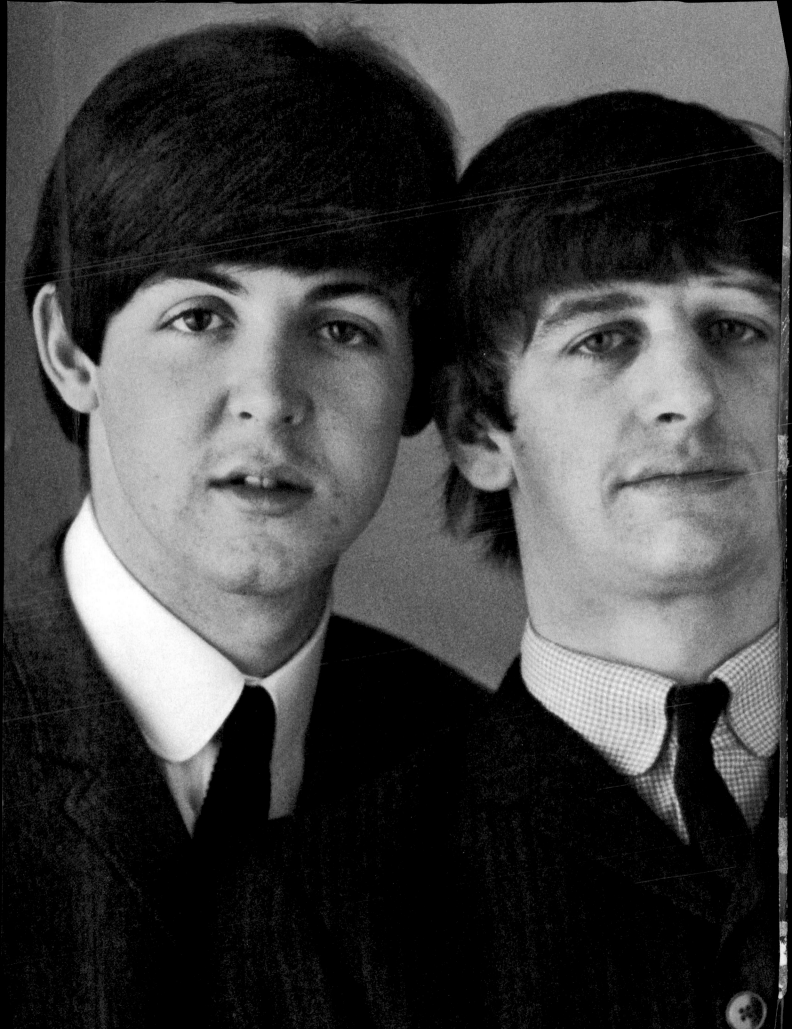

LIFE BOOKS

Managing Editor Robert Sullivan
Director of Photography Barbara Baker Burrows
Creative Director Anke Stohlmann
Deputy Picture Editor Christina Lieberman
Writer-Reporter Marilyn Fu
Copy Editors Barbara Gogan, Parlan McGaw
Consulting Picture Editors Mimi Murphy (Rome),
Tala Skari (Paris)

Editorial Director Stephen Koepp

EDITORIAL OPERATIONS

Richard K. Prue (Director), Brian Fellows (Manager),
Keith Aurelio, Charlotte Coco, Tracey Eure, Kevin
Hart, Mert Kerimoglu, Rosalie Khan, Patricia Koh,
Marco Lau, Brian Mai, Po Fung Ng, Rudi Papiri,
Robert Pizaro, Barry Pribula, Clara Renauro,
Katy Saunders, Hia Tan, Vaune Trachtman

TIME HOME ENTERTAINMENT

Publisher Richard Fraiman
Vice President, Business Development & Strategy
Steven Sandonato
Executive Director, Marketing Services Carol Pittard
Executive Director, Retail & Special Sales Tom Mifsud
Executive Director, New Product Development
Peter Harper
Director, Bookazine Development & Marketing
Laura Adam
Publishing Director Joy Butts
Finance Director Glenn Buonocore
Associate Director, Marketing and Communications
Malati Chavali
Assistant General Counsel Helen Wan
Book Production Manager Suzanne Janso
Design & Prepress Manager Anne-Michelle Gallero
Brand Manager Roshni Patel

Special thanks:

Christine Austin, Jeremy Biloon, Jim Childs,
Susan Chodakiewicz, Jacqueline Fitzgerald,
Carrie Hertan, Christine Font, Lauren Hall,
Malena Jones, Mona Li, Robert Marasco,
Kimberly Marshall, Amy Migliaccio, Dave
Rozzelle, Ilene Schreider, Adriana Tierno, Alex
Voznesenskiy, Jonathan White, Vanessa Wu

Page I Robert Whitaker
Previous spread Jean-Marie Perier/Photo 12/Polaris
This spread Philip Jones Griffiths/Magnum

LIFE

Remembering
GEORGE HARRISON
10 YEARS LATER

Remembering
GEORGE

Ten years ago and much too soon, we lost a second Beatle—a wonderful musician and a wonderful man. Here is George's life, in words and, then, in pictures.

He was "the quiet Beatle" only in that he was standing alongside two louder-than-life characters and in front of a guy playing drums. He held many strong opinions—on Beatlemania, on global want, on his right to privacy, on his God—and gave firm voice to most of them. As a visibly moved Paul McCartney said 10 years ago when his "brother" passed away, George Harrison was a lovely person, possessed of a wicked sense of humor, but one who "did not suffer fools gladly." This man who would happily (and sometimes not so happily) goof around with his mates during the halcyon days, and would later come to embody the ideas of Flower Power and peace on earth, took life very, very seriously, and cherished the personal life deeply.

To that point: Whether or not the quietest Beatle, George was certainly the most reluctant, wanting out almost as soon as he was in. He often said that his luckiest break was joining the band and his second luckiest was leaving it. "Being a Beatle was a nightmare," he said once, "a horror story. I don't even like to think about it." He never really looked comfortable in his tight suit and pudding-basin haircut, not even in the funfest *A Hard Day's Night* (although he met his future wife Pattie Boyd on the set); and in this he was perhaps the most honest Beatle, the one least convincing when wearing the mask. The standard line is that John was cerebral, Paul was cute, Ringo was funny and George was an enigma. But perhaps he was transparent: a terrific guitarist, a fine songwriter, a wonderer, a seeker and, overriding all, a celebrity who hated and feared celebrity.

He died at a friend's home in Los Angeles 10 years ago, in late 2001, at age 58, losing his last battle with cancer. In 1997, he had had a cancerous lump removed from his neck; earlier in '01 he had been operated on for a cancer found on his lung and subsequently received treatment for a tumor on his brain, including a controversial form of radiation therapy at the Staten Island University Hospital in New York City. Harrison's passing left only Paul McCartney and Ringo Starr as surviving members of the Fab Four, John Lennon having been murdered in New York City in 1980.

Harrison's wife, Olivia, and son, Dhani, then 23, were at his bedside when he died; and as word spread about his death, Harrison was mourned and eulogized by the crowds who gathered outside the Abbey Road studios in London and in Strawberry Fields—the area of Manhattan's Central Park across the street from where Lennon was shot—and by his former bandmates. "He was a beautiful man. He was like my baby brother to me," said Sir Paul, who had already lost his wife, Linda, to breast cancer in 1998. Starr, long Harrison's best friend in the band, said, "We will miss George for his sense of love, his sense of music and his sense of laughter."

That hosannas from the knighted would be sung for George Harrison, born the son of a Liverpool bus driver and a shop assistant during the darkest days of World War II, is in keeping with the kind of miracles the Beatles made for themselves. The baby was delivered on February 25, 1943, in a small brick dwelling at 12 Arnold Grove—a "two-up, two-down" townhouse, heated by a single coal fire and with an outhouse in the back—where George would spend his first six years. In Britain's gray but grateful postwar era, the Harrisons were offered a council house at 25 Upton Green, Speke, and life brightened marginally. George attended Dovedale Primary School, where a lad named Lennon—unknown to him—had passed through a couple of years earlier. A bit of trivia: Dovedale Primary is hard by Penny Lane (but then again, that was one of Paul's songs, wasn't it?).

George, by contrast with John and many other eventual British Invasion rock stars, was a fine student early on, and not what might be called "disaffected." If he would eventually become famous for his adherence to Eastern spirituality, he was raised a Roman Catholic, and a good boy. Having passed his grammar school exams with flying colors, he was admitted to the Liverpool Institute High School for

Hamburg, Germany, during the Beatles' first trip, 1960.

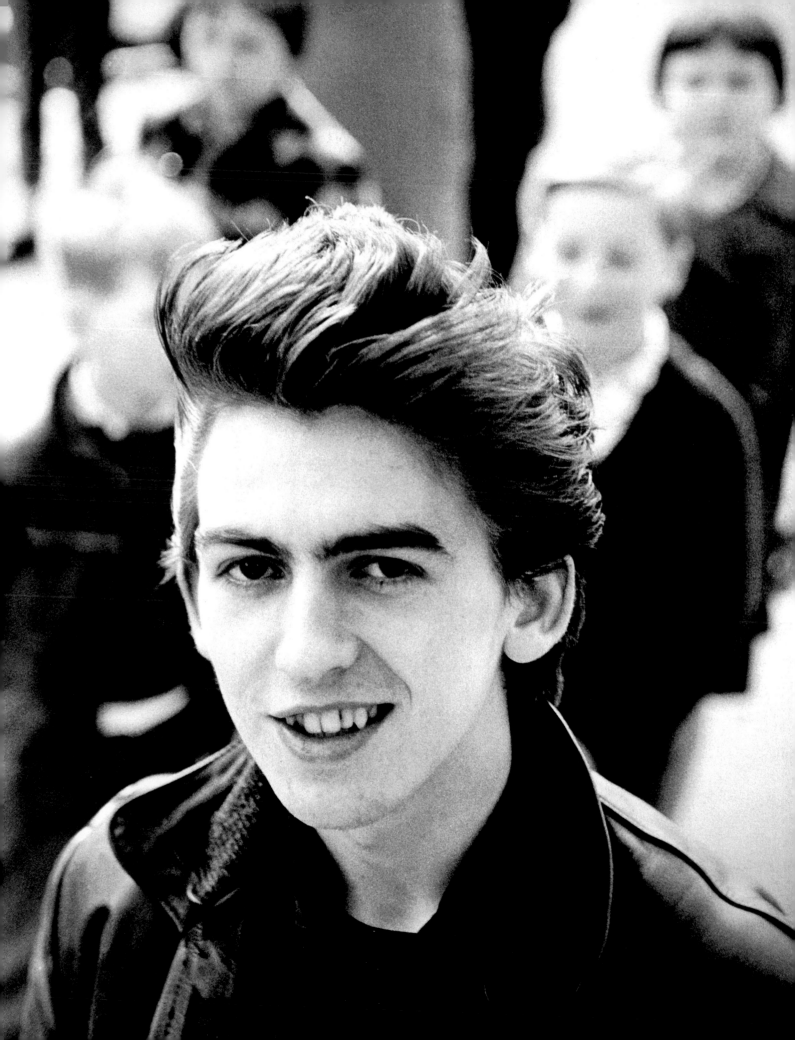

Boys. Then, in 1956, rock 'n' roll—and one song in particular, it seems—swept through the adolescent landscape.

George said later that he heard Elvis Presley's "Heartbreak Hotel" wafting through the windows of a neighborhood house, and nearly lost control of his bicycle. Interestingly, in his lauded 2010 autobiography, *Life,* the Rolling Stones guitarist Keith Richards, whose mother had earlier brought Fats Domino and Big Bill Broonzy music into her household, remembered that it was hearing "Heartbreak Hotel" faintly from Radio Luxembourg that set him upon his mission. John Lennon, too, once reminisced, "When I heard 'Heartbreak Hotel,' I thought, 'this is it' and I started to grow sideboards and all that gear." The song, he said, made his "hair stand on end."

For George's part, he was thoroughly and forever ruined by his Elvis epiphany. He passed his progress tests again and was admitted to the city's best high school, but now he was drawing pictures of guitars in his notebooks when he was supposed to be paying attention. "I was totally into guitars. I heard about this kid who had a guitar for 3 pounds, 10 shillings, it was just a little acoustic round hole. I got the three pounds, 10 shillings from my mother. That was a lot of money for us then." He formed a skiffle group with his brother and a pal (skiffle being a rough British amalgamation of bluegrass, rockabilly and jugband music). They called themselves the Rebels, though they were hardly that. Another, better skiffle band in town was called the Quarry Men, and was fronted by Lennon. In this period, John had allowed into the Quarry Men a fellow named Paul McCartney—and even this was all about the recent "Heartbreak Hotel" tsunami. John initially worried that Paul, so obviously talented and charismatic, might threaten his leadership, but he eventually felt: "The decision was to let Paul in and make the group stronger. He was good. He also looked like Elvis."

The most famous of the Beatles' fated hookups is certainly the one that involves Paul wandering

At the Top Ten Club, on the Reeperbahn in Hamburg, June 1961.

JURGEN VOLLMER/REDFERNS/GETTY

by a summer festival at St. Peter's Church in Liverpool's Woolton district on that hot day in 1957, and being transfixed by the Quarry Men. Paul happened to have brought his guitar and impressed the band's leader with raucous renderings of Eddie Cochran and Little Richard songs. So he was in, and that's the big cosmic moment. Okay.

But in official Beatles lore there's an even earlier bit of destiny. It is back in 1955, and George Harrison, just 12 and not yet totally destroyed by "Heartbreak Hotel," is a student putting in an hour's commute on his dad's bus, traveling from the family home in Speke to the Liverpool Institute. He is engaged in conversation by a boy a year ahead of him in the same school, the son of a cotton salesman from Allerton. Paul McCartney is already crazy about guitars and American rockabilly stars, and soon he is joining young George in the evenings to practice their distinctive versions of "Don't You Rock Me Daddy-O" and "Besame Mucho." Then came Elvis.

Paul, having been accepted into the Quarry Men, told John about his young friend George, who, Paul said, could play the American instrumental hit "Raunchy"—legendarily the first rockabilly song to feature a twangy solo guitar lead—note for note. George's audition for John came atop a double-decker bus, and John was duly impressed, though he was concerned that the boy was simply too young to be part of a band. George hung around like an eager puppy, filling in with the Quarry Men whenever he could, and finally John fell back on his earlier rationale: Make the band better, and repercussions be damned. George was in at age 15. A lovely footnote: When working on the *Beatles Anthology* project in 1994, surviving bandmates Paul, George and Ringo convened at one point at George's grand estate at Friar Park for reminiscence and easy jamming. One tune they revisited, and you can find the happy performance on YouTube, has George playing lead on "Raunchy." As the title of George's tribute song for John upon Lennon's murder in 1980 would observe: "All Those Years Ago." Indeed.

Without rehashing the many permutations of the evolving Quarry Men of the late '50s—the Moondogs, the Silver Beatles, the exploding drummers—we arrive in the Reeperbahn, the famous cabaret district in Hamburg, Germany, in the early 1960s, with a band whose front line is Lennon-McCartney-Harrison. This is because Lennon, in his wisdom (and as mentioned, twice), has decided that he will put at risk his dominance to build the strongest group. Paul was Ingredient A, George is now Ingredient B and before too many more months were passed, Ringo would be C. The way to think of those early Beatles in Hamburg, when Stu Sutcliffe was a fifth member before his untimely death and Pete Best was the drummer of the moment, is as one of the grittiest, nastiest, best punk bands ever, getting tighter by the night during sets that might last eight hours. "We were frothing at the mouth," George remembered in *The Beatles Anthology,* the coffee table scrapbook of photos and reminiscences published in 2000 to accompany the film documentary as well as multiple CD releases, "because we had all these hours to play and the club owners were giving us Preludins, which were slimming tablets. I don't think they were amphetamine, but they were uppers. So we used to be up there foaming, stomping away." On many occasions he said that the best Beatles shows ever had been performed in the clubs of Hamburg.

Obviously if George was in Hamburg in 1960, he wasn't in school. He had dropped out at age 16 to pursue his passion and his dream, with the prosaic day-to-day including an apprenticeship as an electrician at a Liverpool department store. Soon, the Beatles—whether they were called that yet or not quite yet—were his life. At the Kaiserkeller, particularly during the band's second German sojourn in 1961, they played on their own and in conjunction with the English rock 'n' roll singer Tony Sheridan. This historic collaboration produced some cuts under Sheridan's name ("My Bonnie" became a hit in Germany and Great Britain) and a few under the Beatles' new and everlasting imprimatur ("Ain't She Sweet" is perhaps the best remembered). Sheridan, a wizened 21-year-old, cottoned to George, and gave him guitar lessons, which many musicologists credit

Hamburg again, in April 1962.

as contributing greatly to the Beatles' sound. The prevalent theory is that the Beatles helped Tony Sheridan become an eternally famous figure, but perhaps this worked both ways.

George was the baby of the band, and if the inner dynamic of the Beatles had been different, his age might have cost him his place in the legend about to unfold—he could have become a footnote, joining Sheridan and Best and the ill-fated Sutcliffe and John's earlier Quarry Men mates. During the Beatles' first five-month gig in Germany, authorities discovered that Harrison, just turned 17, was too young to be working in the Reeperbahn nightclubs. They had him deported. Guitarists can be replaced, but by then McCartney and Lennon were protective of their little brother—the Beatles were as much a fiercely insular family as they were a ferocious rock band, and they would remain such, even when fracturing in the late '60s; "George has a lot with the others that I can never know about," said Pattie at one point. "Nobody, not even the wives can break through or even comprehend it"—and a few weeks later the boys were playing together again in England. Sounding better than ever, and much better than other Liverpool pop bands, the Beatles became local legends through their shows at the Cavern Club. They got a manager, Brian Epstein, in December of 1961. He got them a record contract with EMI, and a new look: collarless suit jackets and proper (if coolly thin) neckties replacing the black leather of Hamburg. Their producer at EMI, George Martin, quickly opined that the drummer, Best, wasn't the best, and it fell to Epstein to boot Pete out. He was replaced with the talented Ringo, already the star of another Liverpool band, and the lads were on their way. Their first single, "Love Me Do," reached number 17 in Britain in the fall of 1962, and early the following year the LP *Please Please Me* was released.

Everything was happening very, very fast now. Each morning brought new news, a higher chart position, a louder frenzy, a latest target. The Beatles would conquer France, and while there would look to America, thence: the whole world. It was just what John and Paul had always dreamed of, and young George had never dared to imagine.

F or George, much more quickly than for the others, whatever magic there was in the initial moment flickered and died. "At first we all thought we wanted the fame and that," he said in 1988. "After a bit we realized that fame wasn't really what we were after at all, just the fruits of it. After the initial excitement and thrill had worn off, I, for one, became depressed. Is this all we have to look forward to in life? Being chased around by a crowd of hooting lunatics from one crappy hotel room to the next?"

During the Beatles' grand conquest of America in 1964, when their initial appearance on *The Ed Sullivan Show* drew an astonishing 73 million viewers and made them an overnight phenomenon throughout the land, Harrison spent his days in New York City holed up in the Plaza Hotel with a high fever while the Fab Other Three paraded around town, wowing the world's press with their vitality and wit. Then it was on to Washington, D.C., for a concert at the Coliseum before more than 7,000 screaming fans. "It was bloody awful," Harrison told biographer Geoffrey Giuliano. "Some journalist had apparently dug up an old quote of John's that I was fond of jelly babies and had written about it in his column. That night we were absolutely pelted . . . Imagine waves of rock-hard little bullets raining down on you from the sky. Every now and then one would hit a string on my guitar and plonk off a bad note as I was trying to play. From then on, everywhere we went it was exactly the same."

George's guitar idols had included not only rocker Carl Perkins but also Andrés Segovia, and he had worked hard to master an intricate, precise technique (his later experiments with 12-string guitars, not to mention his sitar playing, would be vastly influential in rock music). Now concertgoers couldn't even hear him, and, worse, they didn't care. Harrison, who turned 21 just after that first brief American tour, marveled to the others on the flight home, "How [expletive] stupid it all is. All that big hassle to make it, only to end up as performing fleas."

Yes, sure, difficult, awful—but certainly there were compensations? First, each of the bandmates was soon on the road to being very

In London's Chiswick Park in 1966, by which point George wanted a way out of Beatlemania.

rich, and each was able to do well by the now proud but still working-class parents and relations who remained back in Liverpool. Council house living was replaced by afternoon tea on "estates." Awards were bestowed. In 1965, during the Queen's Birthday Honours program, George and his friends were made members of the Order of the British Empire, and all of them (even John!) professed to be pleased. Then, too, George met his first wife thanks to being a Beatle. Pattie Boyd was a blue-eyed 19-year-old model when she was cast as a schoolgirl fan of the Beatles in *A Hard Day's Night*. George asked her out and she refused him, since she had a serious boyfriend at the time. George asked her out again and—the boyfriend suddenly gone, imagine that!—she accepted. They went to the private Garrick Club in London's Covent Garden, chaperoned after a fashion by Brian Epstein. By December of 1965, the two were engaged, then married within a month. (Pattie was the British Invasion's preeminent siren, Marianne Faithfull and Anita Pallenberg included in the discussion. Lennon, too, fell for Pattie; Mick Jagger took an unsuccessful shot at one point; and she eventually married Eric Clapton after splitting from Harrison. But she always maintained, and maintains today, that George was the most beautiful man she ever met, and he remained the love of her life.)

For all the high times, it wasn't long before the other Beatles shared George's opinion about the insanity of life on the road—indeed, life anywhere in the open—and the band's last public concert was at San Francisco's Candlestick Park on August 29, 1966. To watch video or look at stills from that night is revelatory; the boys proceed with their heads down, even as they produce the goods from the stage. They were terrified by the crush of Beatlemaniacs and were thinking not only of John F. Kennedy's assassination, and what they saw as the relative craziness of America, but also of death threats the Beatles had received in the wake of Lennon's recent "We're more popular than Jesus" comment. George was prepared to not go on at all, but he did. And then that was that.

With the end of live performance, the band, and George in particular, moved on to what he considered more serious endeavors. His marriage to Pattie in early '66 had altered his perspective, as had what he referred to as "the dental experience," which, he said, "made us see life in a different light."

The dental experience had happened back in 1965. Hamburg club managers had introduced the Beatles to uppers, and Bob Dylan had turned them on to marijuana. Now, at a dinner party at George's dentist's house in London, the host slipped sugar cubes laced with LSD into the after-dinner coffee of George and Pattie and John and his wife, Cynthia. Initial anger at what had happened wore off, and within months, all the Beatles were experimenting with acid. Eventually, Paul got into cocaine, John into heroin and George became a fan of hashish (for which he would be busted in March 1969). The music they continued to make in the studio changed. It got denser, trippier. The single "Strawberry Fields" was followed by the seminal album *Sgt. Pepper's Lonely Hearts Club Band*, and the Beatles led their generation into a psychedelic world. As Harrison began to emerge as a songwriter, his exquisitely arranged compositions—"Within You, Without You," "Love You To," "Blue Jay Way"—were informed not only by drug use but also, in their melody and message, by his increasing interest in Eastern religion, culture and music.

He came by this interest, which would become the driving force in his life, in myriad and diverse ways, via very different roads and avenues. Pattie was into Eastern mysticism, and certainly that was a catalyst. Also, George— more than and before his fellow Beatles—was swayed by the folk-rock music of Dylan and the Byrds, and conversations with David Crosby of that wonderful California band led to George's consideration of Indian music, his cognizance of Ravi Shankar and his experiments with the sitar. As all this was happening, the script of the second Beatles film, *Help!*, called for chase scenes involving cartoonish Hindu villains, and Indian sitar players were brought in to provide some zippy chase music. George started noodling on a sitar—if indeed one can noodle on a sitar—and asking questions. This led to exotic instrumentation on the Lennon ballad

Looking past the Beatles, circa 1969.

"Norwegian Wood (This Bird Has Flown)" and later to an apprenticeship with master sitarist Shankar, who gave George lessons on the instrument and in life itself. "He was a friend, a disciple and son to me," said Shankar, whose daughters, Norah Jones and Anoushka Shankar, would become musical stars themselves (and by extension, under Shankar's thinking, George's half-sisters). "George was a brave and beautiful soul, full of love, childlike humor and a deep spirituality." Shankar was with his friend 10 years ago, as George was passing away: "We spent the day before with him, and even then he looked so peaceful, surrounded by love."

The Beatles' famous trip to India in 1968, where they meditated under the guidance of the Maharishi Mahesh Yogi, was largely Harrison's show. He and Pattie had become devotees of the religious leader and they arranged for the band to spend time at the Maharishi's ashram in the Himalayan foothills. Other celebrities—the actress Mia Farrow, the singer Donovan, Mike Love of the Beach Boys—went on retreat as well, and the episode is remembered as one of the pivotal, if oddest, events of the Flower Power '60s.

The band's dynamic had been completely altered, though the four principals remained close. George "was like a disciple of mine when we started," Lennon once said, describing their relationship as "one of young follower and older guy." Said Ringo: "We really looked out for each other and we had so many laughs together. In the old days we'd have the biggest hotel suites, the whole floor of the hotel, and the four of us would end up in the bathroom, just to be with each other . . . There were some really loving, caring moments between four people: a hotel room here and there—a really amazing closeness. Just four guys who loved each other. It was pretty sensational."

But those days were over, or were seriously on the wane. John was now following George to India and into the mystical realm—mentee rather than mentor—and all four Beatles were looking outward more than into the band. Brian Epstein died at age 32 in August 1967 of a drug overdose when the Beatles were away in Bangor, Wales, for a first audience with the Maharishi, who counseled them in their grief that their manager's "death, being within the direct realm of the physical world, is not important." This kind of thinking made more of an impression on George than it did on his friends, but still, they all gave it a try—they were so confused by celebrity, money and drugs, they had become seekers once more, if in a much different and even more desperate way than they had been in Liverpool or Hamburg. Eventually, John in particular shucked the Maharishi and his messages, and denounced him publicly. George remained dedicated to transcendentalism the rest of his days.

Indisputably beautiful fruits of the 1968 getaway were the songs composed there. John said he wrote "hundreds"; Paul came up with at least 15; and most of the Beatles' *White Album* and *Abbey Road* was conceived at the Maharishi's ashram in Rishikesh, India. George contributed a half-dozen songs, including the anti-carnivore screed "Piggies" and the gorgeous "Here Comes the Sun" and "Something." With more than 150 versions recorded, "Something" is the second-most-covered Beatles song after "Yesterday," but a measure of George's obscurity within the band is that Frank Sinatra used to introduce "Something" as his favorite Lennon-McCartney tune. But Sinatra, an expert in other ways, also said "Something" was one of the very best songs written in the previous quarter century.

The so-called *White Album,* actually entitled *The Beatles,* which featured four Harrison compositions, is an extraordinary document. A double album brimful with genius of all sorts, it was rendered in many sessions during which a Beatle or two or maybe three would drop by the Abbey Road studios and lay down a track. Harmonies would be built when they could be, but so inharmonious was the band that walkouts were commonplace. Ringo quit altogether at one point, and George wanted to follow him. Flowers were proffered when everyone came back together. The *Let It Be* film documents much of this, and while the brilliant, consummate album *Abbey Road* stands in lovely counterpoint to the dissonance— George Martin's great effort to reassemble the

In 1970, as he crafts *All Things Must Pass.*

EVERETT

Beatles and do one more like the old days, when they sang and played together—the end was near. In fact, it was at hand.

John left in 1969, and for George, the formal split, announced in 1970, opened the door to artistic liberation. He had been piling up songs for months—years—songs that couldn't be squeezed onto Beatles albums, stuffed as they were with Lennon's and McCartney's efforts. "Until this year," Paul told John in 1969, "our songs have been better than George's. Now this year his songs are at least as good as ours." He was right, and now, in a work that is the very definition of magnum opus, George poured forth the three-disc set *All Things Must Pass.* The bulky boxed set went to No. 1 in 1971, propelled by such hits as "My Sweet Lord" and "What Is Life." The Beatles hadn't deemed "Isn't It a Pity" worthy, if that can be believed. George had found a new spiritual mentor, Srila Prabhupada of the International Society for Krishna Consciousness, and Hindu sentiments and sounds permeated the record, further spurring sitar sales and causing many listeners to investigate Eastern religions.

In the early aftermath of the Beatles' demise, George, the revelation, rivaled John or Paul as a pop icon, and Shankar realized that his friend might be the perfect front man for a good cause. In August 1971, Harrison and associates Dylan, Starr, Clapton and Leon Russell staged two concerts at New York City's Madison Square Garden to raise money for the flood- and famine-ravaged nation to India's east. The Concert for Bangladesh, drawing more than 40,000 fans in all, established George as a pioneering rock philanthropist, and set a model for future celebrity fund-raising efforts like Live Aid, the "We Are the World" record and the Concert for New York City, starring Paul McCartney, which was staged at Madison Square Garden for victims of the World Trade Center attacks—staged barely more than a month before Paul's "little brother" passed away. It is impossible to estimate how many of the world's disadvantaged people have been benefited by the efforts of George Harrison. Later, when he was rarely appearing onstage, he still made surprise performances, at such as the Birmingham Heartbeat 86 charity

concert (1986) to sing "Johnny B. Goode" or the Prince's Trust concert (1987) to perform "While My Guitar Gently Weeps" and "Here Comes the Sun" alongside Ringo and Eric Clapton. On April 6, 1992, he performed his last complete concert and his first in London in 23 years at a benefit for the Natural Law Party.

With the Beatles disbanded in the 1970s and George now front and center, his fans got to know him better. It became evident that the quiet Beatle was, in fact, possessed of the same dry, sarcastic, Liverpudlian wit that John was known for. (During the Beatles' recording session with George Martin back in 1962, the producer asked them, "Is there anything you're not happy about?" It was George, not John, after all, who famously answered, "Well, there's your tie, for starters.") George, with individual success, seemed more at ease, and in his geniality his image evolved to that of the happy mystic.

Clapton, along with Dylan, became one of Harrison's best friends, and it's rather astonishing that this friendship was not destroyed when Pattie became Mrs. Clapton in 1979, two years after she and George divorced and a year after George married the American Olivia Arias. (A marriage that saddened Pattie, regretful as she was that she and George hadn't lasted.) In 1991, Eric and George worked Japan together as a double bill—George's last-ever megatour.

By the late 1970s, George was as much entrepreneur as musician. He had started his own record label (Dark Horse, in 1974) and his own movie production company, HandMade Films, which he set up to help his pal Eric Idle finish his Monty Python film *Life of Brian.* Other HandMade productions included the 1981 fantasy *Time Bandits* and the 1986 noirish drama *Mona Lisa.* George's cinema dabblings also included a cameo in Idle's faux rockumentary, *All You Need Is Cash,* about the Rutles—the "Prefab Four." According to George, the parody told the Beatles' story "much better than the usual boring documentary."

Scared into near reclusion by Mark David Chapman's killing of Lennon in December 1980, George spent most of his time meditating, music making, gardening and watching Formula One races on the telly at Friar Park, his

The happy mystic in the 1970s.

extraordinary estate in Henley-on-Thames, and at his hideaway on the Hawaiian island of Maui. As we've said, he ventured out occasionally (and often unannounced) to play, especially for good causes, and he recorded as a solo act and also with the Traveling Wilburys, a supergroup that included Bob Dylan, Tom Petty, Roy Orbison and Jeff Lynne. But various legal battles took up even more of his time. In 1976, he had to pay hundreds of thousands of dollars for "subconsciously plagiarizing" the old Chiffons hit "He's So Fine" in his melody for "My Sweet Lord." In 1991, he brought a seven-figure defamation-of-character suit when the tabloid the *Globe* published a story calling him a "Big Nazi Fan." (The lawsuit reportedly resulted in a sizable out-of-court settlment for George.) And in 1996, he won an $11.6 million judgment against his former business partner in HandMade films.

That same year, Harrison asked authorities to investigate a series of death threats. None of those threats were proved to have come from Michael Abram, but it was Abram, a 33-year-old Beatle obsessive from a Liverpool suburb, who, in the dead of night on December 30, 1999, got past the alarms and razor wire at Friar Park and broke into the Harrisons' mansion. George suffered an inch-deep stab wound to his chest before Olivia knocked Abram down with a bedside lamp. George recovered, and Abram was sent to a mental institution.

While George was able—barely—to survive the pressures of being a Beatle and a violent assault, he couldn't beat cancer. But he made the passage to death easier for himself by believing so passionately for so long in a life after this one. Said his old friend Mia Farrow, who had sat cross-legged and peaceful beside George in India all those years ago, upon hearing of his death: "One of the things that was so inspiring was his lifelong search to know his God. And if God exists, I don't doubt that George has a place near him."

If she's right, Harrison is happy. He may have been scared by the adoring crowds—he might have been scared of many things—but he was not afraid to let go.

At home at Friar Park, in Henley-on-Thames, in 1987.

REX/EVERETT

Joining
JOHN'S BAND

The bus driver's boy falls in league with a pair of like-thinking Liverpool lads, and everything changes—oh so very quickly.

ON THE previous page we see young George with his mates—his bandmates—John Lennon and Paul McCartney outside the McCartney family's house in Liverpool on August 9, 1961, several months before everything took off. An even younger George, with his brother Peter, is seen at left in both of the photos on this page.

EVERETT (2)

GEORGE, age 8 in 1951, is front and center above, flanked by his parents, Harold and Louise. His brothers, Harold (left, age 17, better known as Harry) and Peter (11), are standing. The Harrison boys were tight-knit, and would remain so (George's brothers later were employed at his Friar Park estate; George wouldn't speak to his older sister, Louise, not pictured here, for six years after she became affiliated with a bed-and-breakfast called Hard Day's Nite in Illinois, although these siblings too reconciled before his death). George was close to his parents as well, and remembered a school incident from this exact period in his memoir *I Me Mine*: "Once when I was eight or nine years old, Mr. Lyons (brother of the local insurance salesman) a teacher, caned me and got me on the wrist. It was swollen and when I got home, I tried to hide it but my father saw it and the next day he came down to the school and Mr. Lyons was called out of the class and my dad 'stuck one' on him." On the following pages, from left, Paul, John and George are the front line—and, truly, the goods—of John's band on December 20, 1958, when they perform at brother Harry's wedding reception at the Childwall Abbey Hotel in Liverpool. "My attitude to playing in the band was that that was the good part of life, that was what it was all about," George recalled of this period in his autobiography. "Definitely the most pleasurable time."

WHEN YOU'RE playing eight hours a night, sometimes you must sit down, and here we see Stuart Sutcliffe (left) and George during a set at the Top Ten Club in Hamburg in 1961. Sutcliffe is certainly among the most interesting of all the so-called "Fifth Beatles." Not only was he truly in the band, he was a riveting and important presence. Better looking than even Paul, he was, in Hamburg, the band's original rock star. "Stuart was cool," George said in *The Beatles Anthology*. "He was great looking and had a great vibe about him, and was a very friendly bloke. I liked Stuart a lot, he was always very gentle." Sutcliffe played bass at the time, but took to George and, as Tony Sheridan did in this same period, worked with the teenager on guitar technique. Sutcliffe, an aspirant painter, had been brought into the band by his friend Lennon, but quite quickly George was his confrere—and protégé. Sutcliffe was not long for the Beatles, but he was important. His girlfriend Astrid Kirchherr, a stylish young photographer, influenced their leather-clad look in the Hamburg years, and after Stuart asked Astrid to cut his hair a certain way, the Beatles' famous moptop look was born. Sutcliffe was a so-so musician and an ambivalent Beatle, remaining behind in Hamburg with Astrid (to whom he would become engaged) even as the group's upward trajectory in England began. John and George, in particular, were dismayed by this. Paul switched from joint rhythm guitar (with John) to bass guitar, and the band became a four-piece. And then, in Germany, Stuart died of a brain hemorrhage. This was an early wake-up call for the Beatles about life itself, and a shock for George—not yet 20.

MARK & COLLEEN HAYWARD/REDFERNS/GETTY

IN LIVERPOOL in 1961 and '62, the Cavern Club was the scene, not least because that's where the Beatles were. "It was still a jazz place," George remembered in *The Beatles Anthology* of the time of their first gigs there, "and they tried to kick us off, because we were rock 'n' roll." The Cavern's attitude changed as the receipts piled up thanks to the Beatles, and they were the reason that record store impresario Brian Epstein chose to visit one day, was duly impressed, signed the band and started plotting their mutual future. The photos at top left and bottom are from 1962, and the one at top right was taken at the Cavern in November of 1961. The girls are already glomming on to Paul, John is rising above, George is a little shy—and there's an interesting blond fellow, on the right, having a cuppa. He is Rory Storm, and therein lie two or three tales. First, one of George's earliest girlfriends was Rory's sister Iris, who was 12 when she palled around with George and 17 when she liked Paul. Second, Rory was a lead singer and a friendly rival of the Beatles in the Hamburg/Liverpool/Cavern Club years, and his drummer in Rory Storm and the Hurricanes was Richard Starkey, who evolved in this period into Ringo Starr. George was instrumental in having John and Paul tilt toward Ringo, and after recording with him in Hamburg the Beatles played dates at the Cavern Club with him when Pete Best was sick. According to Brian Epstein's autobiography, Rory Storm, who died at age 33 in 1972, was, "[O]ne of the liveliest and most likeable young men on the scene." Epstein said further that Storm "was very annoyed when Ringo left and he complained to me. I apologized, and Rory, with immense good humor said, 'Okay. Forget it. The best of luck to the lot of you.'" And off they went.

EVERETT

BRIAN EPSTEIN has signed the group and tidied them up. "People thought we looked undesirable," George remembers in *The Beatles Anthology.* "Even nowadays kids with leather jackets and long hair are seen as apprentice hooligans, but they are just kids, that's the fashion they like—leathers. And it was like that with us. With black T-shirts, black leather gear and sweaty, we did look like hooligans . . . Brian Epstein was from an upper middle-class background and he wanted us to appeal to the producers of radio, television and record companies. We gladly switched into suits to get some more money and some more gigs."

K & K ULF KRUGER/REDFERNS/GETTY

LFI/PHOTOSHOT

THREE PICTURES circa 1962, and yet another Beatles footnote: The piano player rocking with them above is Roy Young, who also sang and was known at the time as "England's Little Richard." Young, who occasionally joined the nascent Beatles onstage at the Star-Club in Hamburg in this period, said that Brian Epstein offered him a place in the band, but that his contractual commitment to the Star-Club precluded him from returning to England. Young continues to perform today, but makes no oversize claims as the Fifth Beatle.

K & K ULF KRUGER/REDFERNS/GETTY

BEATLE MANIA

From the outside, it looked like a blessing. From the inside, it often seemed a curse, particularly to George. But it is undeniable all these years later: It was nothing short of fantastic at the time.

ON THE previous spread, George is on the run, gratefully accepting the helping hand of the constabulary as he flees fans and heads for a concert performance in Scarborough, England, on August 9, 1964. At left he addresses the adoring crowd in Liverpool in 1963, with the omnipresent girls now pressing in as close as they can. In this period, the crush begins, and it will only get more intense—or, in George's view, worse—in the months and years ahead.

THE BEATLES were about many things, and changed many things. They were about music, youth, volume, energy, a postwar changing of the guard. Overnight, they redefined the way kids were supposed to look and feel. At right we see the Fab Four primping before a November 1963 concert at the Coventry Theatre near London (and please note George at the far right of the photograph, taking very seriously the lay of his moptop). Paris was disquieted by this loud volley from London: France had always dictated to the British (and indeed the wider world) when it came to food, wine and fashion. But now miniskirts and a waif named Twiggy and overarchingly the Beatles were calling the tune. If the nexus of the music was Abbey Road, the new style capital was Carnaby Street. Throughout the '60s, John, Paul, George and Ringo would lead their generation (and younger ones) into new looks, colors and modes of expression. But nothing to follow would be as sensational as the first blush of Beatlemania, when girls went crazy for these four rock idols and boys rushed to their local barbershops (below, in London) to get their longer locks trimmed just so.

TERENCE SPENCER (2)

THEY WERE STRUTTING, flying high. They owned London (here) and the Continent, and were soon to conquer the world. "Love Me Do" had crawled up the British charts, but "Please Please Me" rocketed, and quite overnight the Beatles were everywhere in England: *The Friday Spectacular, Saturday Club, Here We Go.* The Liverpool lads had been forced to relocate to the big town, as George recalled in his memoir: "Things happened quickly after we moved to London. Ringo and I moved from the first flat to another, better one downstairs, and then moved to Whaddon House, to the flat below Brian's, because we couldn't get the lease renewed in Green Street because of all the litter caused by fans and because of the fans themselves. The fans, all shapes, all manner of humanity, were everywhere. We couldn't get in and out."

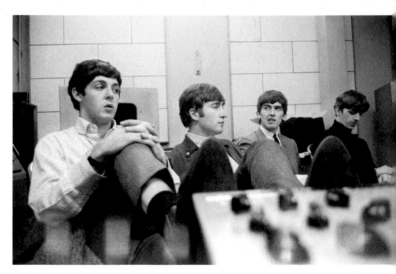

WHAT TO SAY about EMI's studios—better known now and forevermore as "Abbey Road"? This was the Beatles' true home. They occasionally tried to record elsewhere—even in America, in Memphis, during one tour—but because of regulations or missing personnel, nothing came of these other plans, and what we know of Beatles music was made in Abbey Road. "From the early recording sessions they always worked in No. 2 Studio, at Abbey Road," recalled the band's longtime manager, Neil Aspinall, in *The Beatles Anthology*. "There were stairs coming down into the studio, it was a quite big, barn-like room. I know the Beatles were very nervous at first, but then I guess anybody would be at their first recording session." The elder statesman with the blond hair in several of these rarely seen photos from 1963—the fellow who seems to be weighing in—is George Martin (today *Sir* George Martin), the band's producer from the very first and throughout (save *Let It Be*), and as much a deserved claimant to the title Fifth Beatle as even Stuart Sutcliffe or Pete Best. "I had been up to the Cavern and I'd seen what they could do," he reminisced later. "I knew their repertoire, knew what they were able to perform and I said 'Let's record every song you've got; come down to the studios and we'll just whistle through them in a day.' We started about eleven in the morning, finished about eleven at night, and recorded a complete album during that time."

ALREADY HEROES at home, the Beatles quickly conquered Europe before invading America. They recorded German-language versions of their biggest hits to make their fans in Hamburg happy; and here, in January of 1964, they had a grand time on the Champs-Élysées before performing in Paris's Olympia music hall. (Opposite: George is at left as he and Paul take pictures of John—as if more pictures were needed by this point. Above: George has become practiced at multitasking, able to carry on a conversation with John and carry out his duties as a Beatle simultaneously.) During their time in Paris, the Beatles learn that "I Want to Hold Your Hand" has gone to Number One in the United States, and that their pathway to America—thence the wider world—is now paved with gold.

THE BEATLES long lamented that some of the earliest business deals they signed weren't advantageous, but still: The money coming in was so substantial, some of it inevitably trickled down to the boys, and they were able to do good by their parents and for themselves. The bungalow called Kinfauns, at 16 Claremont Drive in Esher, Surrey, was available for £20,000 in 1964, and George (above, that year) was in the mood to buy a house: "It was the first one I saw, thought that'll do." Once he married in 1966, he and his wife, the former Pattie Boyd, called Kinfauns home. Later in the '60s, they took to decorating the place (left and opposite).

IT MIGHT not have been good to draw attention to the house. Besides Paul's place, it was where the Beatles most often convened (many of the demos for the so-called *White Album* were made at Kinfauns), and now it is known that the Lennons (John and Cynthia) and soon-to-be Harrisons (George and Pattie) came down from their first acid trip there in 1965. The Harrisons were subsequently busted for hashish possession at Kinfauns in 1969. Above, right: Meantime in 1964, in a much more wholesome domestic situation, George's parents are at their own home trying to cope with their son's multitudinous 21st-birthday greetings.

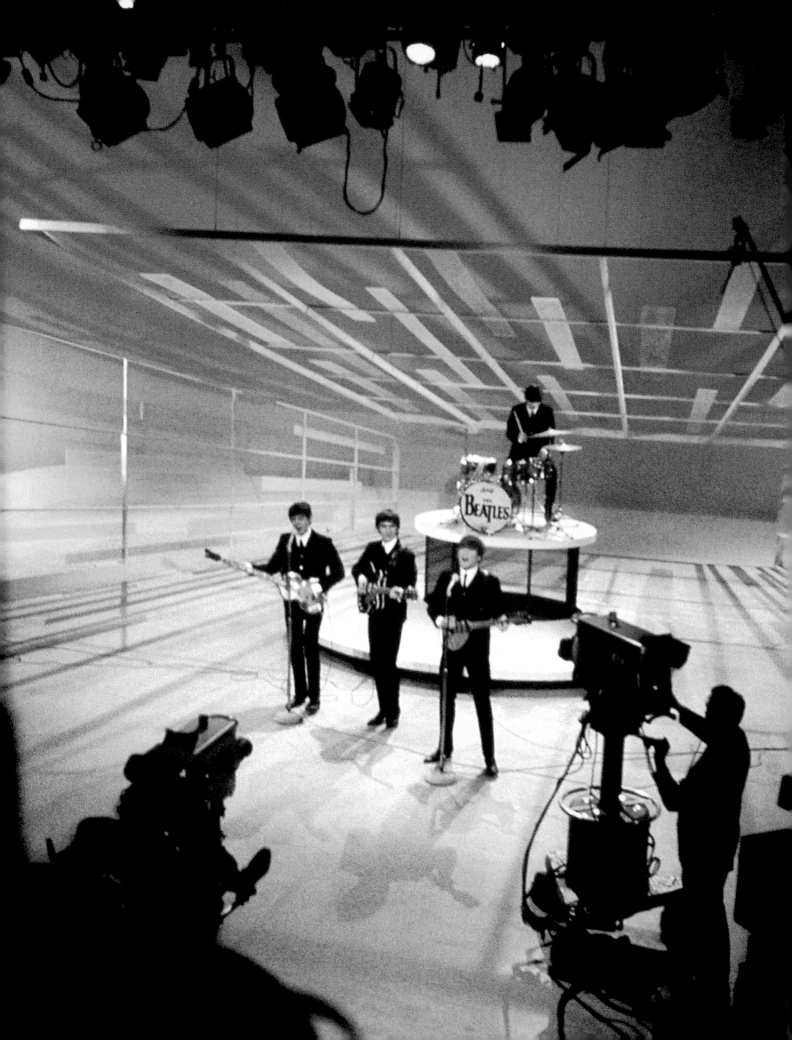

THE BEATLES, the Rolling Stones, the Yardbirds and others had reinterpreted Elvis Presley and American rhythm and blues for an English audience, and now they were bringing their own version to the States in what would be called the British Invasion. They would finally get to meet their idols (below, with Fats Domino) and would reach millions upon millions of fans via *The Ed Sullivan Show* (opposite). George was sick as a dog for much of the first New York visit, and so it was left to his mates to do the publicity shots in Central Park (right) while he convalesced across the road at the Plaza Hotel, saving his energy for the "really big sheeew."

BILL EPPRIDGE (3)

GEORGE WAS feeling much better by the time he boarded the train in New York to go to Washington, D.C., where the Beatles were to play their first big-time concert in the U.S. Also on board was LIFE's Bill Eppridge, who took these three and many other photographs. It is interesting, all these years later, to look at Eppridge's take with George in mind (back in '64, everyone wanted John or Paul pictures, so these are rarely seen photographs). George was very much the kid in the band, the little brother, and was treated—lovingly—as such. He was still struck by it all, and was enthusiastic. He was already smoking too much, and this would become his problem to a larger degree than it was his bandmates'. But it was an effervescent time, and before the jelly beans started plinking off his guitar strings in Washington, George was well into it.

"OBVIOUSLY we were having an effect, because all these people were clamouring to meet us—people like Muhammad Ali," remembered George in *The Beatles Anthology*. "We were taken to meet him on that first trip." Indeed: This was the end of the mad-dash American assault in February of 1964, and *Ed Sullivan* and Washington were in the rear-view mirror and the boys were in Miami where Ali—then still named Cassius Clay—happened to be training for his first heavyweight title bout against Sonny Liston (which Clay would win). Clay, an Olympic champion but hardly yet a media icon, was a severe underdog in the lead-up to the fight, and was happy to boost his public persona by posing for pictures with this latest flavor of the month, the Beatles. "It was a big publicity thing," said George. "It was all part of being a Beatle, really; just getting lugged around and thrust into rooms full of press men taking pictures and asking questions. Muhammad Ali was quite cute." He would remain so, the rest of his days. And because they lasted such a short time and are now preserved in amber, so would the Beatles.

"BEATLES DEPLANING" photos that are usually shown have the band arriving at Idlewild (now JFK) Airport in New York in February of 1964, intent on charming the pants off the press and conquering America. This one is a bit different, and all the more engaging, as it shows the conquering heroes returning to London later that same month with some of the spoils—in vinyl, 33 1/3-rpm form—of their campaign. George is still smiling, but is already wondering what in the world this is all about. He later said of 1964: "On tour that year, it was crazy. Not within the band. In the band we were normal, and the rest of the world was crazy." This dynamic would never change for the Beatles as long as they continued to perform in public. And actually, considering the later attacks on both John and George, even after.

OKAY, OKAY: Stu Sutcliffe was formally the Fifth Beatle for a while; Pete Best was the Fourth Beatle before Ringo took his place and is seen by many, historically, as the Fifth Beatle; George Martin has been called the Fifth Beatle; and we've even mentioned, on page 36, Roy Young as a feasible Fifth. This doesn't even address New York disc jockey Murray the K's eternal Fifth Beatle claim. But wearing the hat, at left, we have the *official* Fifth Beatle; Paul McCartney called him that when he died at age 32 in 1967. This was Brian Epstein, the band's manager who would pass away of an accidental drug overdose. "He dedicated so much of his life to the Beatles," said George. "We liked and loved him. He was one of us." This fun photograph from the Beatles' second U.S. tour in 1964, wherein the musically disinclined Epstein noodles with instruction from George, shows him at his happiest. As George observed after Epstein's death: "Brian hadn't really done anything after we stopped touring. He was at a bit of a loss." Opposite: LIFE was slow on the uptake with the Beatles, as it had been with Elvis in the '50s, but was ready to herald their return to the States in the summer of '64 with a cover portrait by staff photographer John Dominis, who had recently produced a photo essay on Frank Sinatra at age 50 that would become famous when it ran later that same year. The times they were a-changin', and we finally admitted it.

LIFE

THE BEATLES
They're here again
and what a ruckus!

EVERETT

TERENCE SPENCER (3)

THERE IS no way to measure, no way to quantify, Beatlemania. The intensity and pressure were off the charts. Film director Richard Lester did the best possible job of capturing the craziness in the film *A Hard Day's Night* (opposite, top; and this page, top left: three fans at the movie's July 1964 premiere at the London Palladium), but to truly feel it, in 1963 and 1964, one had to be there. British photographer Terence Spencer, who took the remaining four photographs on these pages, was right there, front and center—in the mosh pit, so to speak—and he told LIFE's editors in New York City what was going on, not only throughout Europe but right outside our offices. We liked Terry a lot, and respected his opinion on most occasions, but we ignored him as regarded the Beatles—until we couldn't any longer. On the following pages: During the second U.S. sojourn in '64, when all public spaces were out of the question, George and John warmed up where they could.

THE FILM *A Hard Day's Night* is both a documentary of what was happening to the Beatles in the first half of 1964 and an entertainment depicting that kind of nuttiness. And it is funny and engaging at every turn, whether you're watching for yucks or a slice of life. "We were like that," John once said, while adding that he found the film, nonetheless, "a comic-strip version of what was actually going on." That's about right.

LFI/PHOTOSHOT

DAVID HURN/MAGNUM

OF THE four pictures on these two pages, three are from the film and one is of the boys, guard down, during the making of the film. Can you select the "real" one? Well, we've made it easy for you by saving it for last. On the opposite page are the Beatles running from fans, à la real life but in fact in a scene from *A Hard Day's Night*, and then three of them, still on the run, conversing with one another in the only way possible (ah, an age before cellphones!). On this page, at top, is George rehearsing one of his larkish bits while Ringo and John chat up the women (and we'll get to George chatting up women on the set of *A Hard Day's Night* soon enough). At right are the Beatles on a train that was used for several scenes, but the fans are real, having invaded the set, and the moment is real, too. George's expression, when the movie camera isn't rolling, perhaps says much.

BETTMANN/CORBIS

DAVID HURN/MAGNUM

PATTIE BOYD was a slim young model cast, along with her younger sister Jenny (the inspiration for Donovan's song "Jennifer Juniper"), as Beatles fans in *A Hard Day's Night*. Of course the Boyd girls caught the band's collective eye. As it happened, Pattie already had a thing for George, and he picked up the signals. She later remembered: "When we started filming, I could feel George looking at me, and I was a bit embarrassed." Not so embarrassed that she demurred, however, and after filming, George and Pattie took a holiday with John and his wife, Cynthia, at Dromoland Castle in the west of Ireland. Pattie was quite as of-the-moment as the Beatles were; the even more famous model, Twiggy, borrowed style tips from her. Cynthia later wrote in her memoirs: "Whenever fashions changed [Pattie] was in there first with all the right gear looking beautiful as ever." It's amusing how George and Pattie's courtship so resembled the movie they had just wrapped. In Ireland, their presence was found out by the press, and John and George, to protect the women, flagrantly went to the lobby of Dromoland Castle to check out, hoping Cynthia and Pattie might slip away unnoticed. Pattie later told Beatles biographer Hunter Davies: "In the end Cyn and I had to dress as maids. They took us out a back way, put us in a laundry basket, and we were driven to the airport in a laundry van." The Beatles' first film was minus a great bonus scene.

"AFTER A TIME we moved to Esher because I had to get out of town," George wrote of his and Pattie's domestic relocation, even before they were married, to the house called Kinfauns. "That was when the novelty of being popular wore off." George would be a country mouse, rather than a city mouse, the rest of his days, as Kinfauns would be followed by grander redoubts in rural England and hideaways in Hawaii. He liked nothing better than pottering about the yard; it is telling that his autobiography, which was published in 1980, is "dedicated to gardeners everywhere." Much of the world likes to see its rock stars as nocturnal animals of pale skin and wanton ways. But George was different, and would lead his life in a different way. George was always very, very different.

And In
THE END

As the most beloved band of all time runs out of gas, George sets off on his own—but not without friends, of which there are many, including John, Paul and Ringo. And not without his multitude of devoted fans.

IN THE PICTURE that opens this chapter on the previous spread, George and John duel jocularly in the mid-1960s: a metaphor, surely, for all that was going on with the Beatles. At left John exults during the Shea Stadium concert in New York City on August 15, 1965, and the girls go wild (above). George seems far more wary.

PA/ABACA/POLARIS

IN 1965 the individual Beatles were made members of the Order of the British Empire, the lowest form of knighthood, but a form of knighthood nonetheless (Paul and the band's producer, George Martin, would much later be made true knights—Sir Paul and Sir George. John Lennon and George Harrison died too soon for QE II to do the right thing, and, as usual, Ringo has so far been dissed). During the MBE ceremonies, the bobbies were barely able to keep "the birds" at bay (below).

PA

HULTON-DEUTSCH/CORBIS

THE MOST famous interchange between the Beatles and British royalty has the always cheeky John, presiding from the stage at the Royal Variety Show at the Prince of Wales Theatre in London on November 4, 1963, smiling slyly in the presence of the Queen Mum, Princess Margaret and Margaret's husband, Lord Snowdon, and suggesting: "Would the people in the cheaper seats clap your hands. And the rest of you—if you'd just rattle your jewelry." But our favorite, for the purposes of this book, has George (above, giving a thumbs-up to fans on the hard day of knighting), famished at the *Hard Day's Night* premiere party at the Dorchester Hotel on July 6, 1964, having been told the food simply cannot be rolled out until Margaret and Snowdon have finished with their courtesies. George says to the princess, as delicately as he can: "Your highness, we really are hungry and we can't eat until you two go." The royals, who were actually great friends of George and company, promptly and helpfully depart, stage left. The Beatles subsequently chow down.

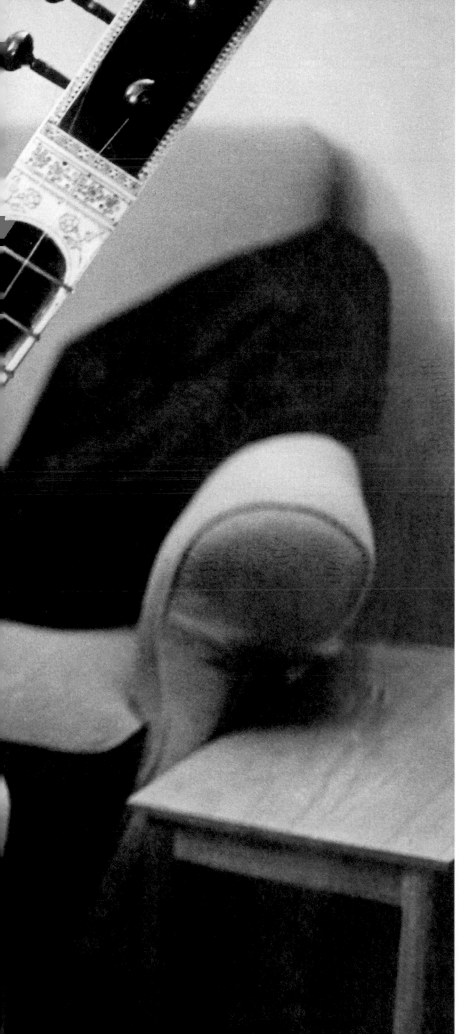

EASTWARD HO! It is a marvelous Beatles footnote, and quite in refutation of the common assumptions, that Pattie Boyd (soon to be Pattie Harrison) was greatly responsible for George's investigations of Eastern mores and music. The chroniclers usually focus on Ravi Shankar or the Maharishi Mahesh Yogi when arriving at this chapter of George's life, but they would do better to look more closely at the pretty London-based model who had captured his heart, and who happened to be fascinated by the ways, whys and wherefores of Eastern spirituality. Pattie would be muse to more than one man—she was, after all, a woman for whom "Something" was written, and also "Layla"—but in the middle 1960s, she was instrumental in stoking George's interest in Indian music and philosophy. It is a very short line from Pattie Boyd, progenitor supermodel and swinging Carnaby Street chick, to the exotic sitar line in "Norwegian Wood" and the thoroughgoing elliptical nature of "Within You Without You." At one point George and Pattie were off to Bombay, where George presented himself as an acolyte to his host, Shankar. "The first time I heard Indian music I felt as though I knew it," he said later. "It was everything, everything I could think of. It was like every music I had ever heard, but twenty times better than everything all put together. It was just so strong, so overwhelmingly positive, it buzzed me right out of my brain." Shankar took George to local temples, gave him books and tutored him during schooldays that, once practice sessions were figured in, might last eight hours. The whole of that trip to India, George said, "was a search for spiritual connection."

IT WAS a strange time and a spiritual time and a mystic time, sure, but it was also a fun time—at least at times. There is some justification in the general objection to any Beatle's later complaint that Beatlemania was nothing but a horrorshow. *Oh, come on, get over it. The world loved you guys, every woman in the world loved you. Why couldn't you just smile and enjoy it, for crying out loud?* And on regular occasion, the boys did smile, as they set to work, in 1965, on their second movie. *Help!*, the exuberant spirit of which (both in front of the camera and behind the scenes) is captured below, at right and on the following two pages. But *Help!* represents, in retrospect, an entirely different irony than *A Hard Day's Night*. That first film was a fictional depiction of a literal and very real (and real-world) craziness. *Help!* was a cartoon narrative that could be enjoyed in full, splashy color as simply a madcap comedy, and, yes, its mood was launched by its propulsive, get-up-and-dance title song, ordered up by director Richard Lester. But that song was one of John's first overtly confessional offerings—or at least John said so later on—and his vocal was as raw and impassioned as anything he had done since "Money" or "Twist and Shout." When he sang "Help, I need somebody/Help, not just anybody," some who were listening could not help but hear him. George was one who certainly did.

"THERE WAS more good than evil in being a Beatle," admitted George in *I Me Mine*, "but it was awful being on the front page of everyone's life, every day . . . [T]he Dick Lester version of our lives in *Hard Day's Night* and *Help!* made it look fun and games: a good romp? That was fair in the films but in the real world there was never any doubt. The Beatles were doomed. Your own space, man, it's so important. That's why we were doomed because we didn't have any. It is like monkeys in a zoo. They die. You know, everything needs to be left alone." George, no great skier, didn't begrudge a frolic in the snow during the filming of *Help!*, and George, certainly no soldier, didn't mind toting a rifle in the movie. But he ultimately felt overwhelmed, like that terrified monkey in the zoo, by life on the road. On the following pages is Jim Marshall's iconic photograph of three guitarists taking the field in San Francisco's Candlestick Park on August 29, 1966, before what would be their final ever public concert as the front line of the Beatles (save, as an asterisk, the rooftop *Let It Be* session in London; please see page 92). John and Paul seem happy enough in the moment. George, certainly, will have no regrets in the morning.

GEORGE AND PATTIE were into all things Indian, and deeply
in love with one another, when they suddenly wed on January 21,
1966, while John and Ringo were on holiday in Trinidad. During the
small ceremony at the Epsom Registry not far from Kinfauns, Brian
Epstein (opposite, far left) and Paul served as joint best men (the senior
Harrisons are immediately behind the happy couple). All the Beatles
were at an early audience with the Maharishi Mahesh Yogi in Wales
in August of 1967 (above) when one of the band's associates, Peter
Brown, called from London and let the phone ring and ring and ring.
Finally Paul's longtime love, Jane Asher (above, far left), picked up, and
Brown said, "Could you find Paul and put him on the phone." Brown
delivered the news that Epstein was dead of a drug overdose. The
Maharishi counseled the grief-stricken young men to let it be: "[Y]ou
have to grieve for him and love him, and now you send him on his way."
John, the chief mouthpiece in this instance (and others), reiterated
such exotic sentiments to the press when they clamored for comment:
"Well, Brian is just passing into the next phase." Later he remembered
knowing, deep down, "we were in trouble," and thinking to himself
much more prosaically: "We've [expletive] had it." George, of course,
was not so convinced—not at the moment—because he had faith in
his new spiritual mentor. But history would prove that the end game
for the Beatles was indeed precipitated by or greatly spurred by Brian
Epstein's passing at age 32.

ED THRASHER/MPTV IMAGES

IN THE latter half of the 1960s, the always trend-setting Beatles existed in a psychedelic, multicolored world that they and their generation reveled in to the max (including, for them, a promo film for the single "Lady Madonna," top). When that world was contrasted with the black-and-white greater universe (as during an audience George and Pattie had with Frank Sinatra, above, during which George could have put Ol' Blue Eyes straight about who actually wrote "Something"), the effect was as surreal as an acid trip—downright alarming. This would have been the point where the Beatles were looking back with longing upon the days when they had actually liked one another, cared about one another, even loved one another like brothers. It would of course be left to John and Paul to formally dissolve the group, but Ringo and George were hardly amused by the fractious *White Album* sessions, and George was certainly frustrated that his increasingly fine output of songs gained too little purchase on Beatles albums. There was only one solution, and the Fab Four were now clearly destined to go off in four different ways. Lamentable, perhaps—but at this stage inevitable.

EVERETT (2)

THE PRODUCER George Martin can and should be credited with many marvelous achievements. Chief among them might be his earnest effort to get the lads back into the studio to record one more album in the manner they had in the old days—with collaboration, collegiality, interplay, harmony. *Abbey Road*, with its famous cover art of the Beatles walking in lockstep toward the studio, could be considered the last of the Beatles' many miracles: a triumphant swan song made even as the ship was sinking. In stark contrast to the sunshine-drenched *Abbey Road* is the tempest that is today remembered as *Let It Be*—which phrase denotes a fine McCartney ballad, an okay LP, a distressing documentary film, a nasty state of mind. The last Beatles album released (and the only one not produced by George Martin; the tapes were sort of thrown at Phil Spector, and Paul for one hated what Spector did to the songs), *Let It Be* was actually recorded *before* the lovely coda that became *Abbey Road* and shortly after the *White Album*.

THE PHOTOGRAPHS on this page reflect the mood of the *Let It Be* sessions—"the low of all time," George later recalled; "hell," said John succinctly—and in his memoir George remembered the entire time well (though not fondly) as "the *Let It Be* fiasco . . . We had been away from each other after having had a very difficult time recording the *White Album*. That double album was so long it went on forever, and there was all kinds of other [expletive] things happening in the band; pressures and problems and after that we came back from a holiday, and went straight back into the old routine. It is that concept of how everybody sees and treats everybody else, allowing no consideration for the fact that we are changing all the time . . . I remember Paul and I were trying to have an argument and the crew carried on filming and recording us. Anyway, after one of those first mornings—I couldn't stand it; I decided this is it!—it's not fun anymore—it's very unhappy being in this band—it's a lot of crap—thank you I'm leaving . . . John and Yoko were freaking out screaming—I'd left the band, gone home—and wrote this tune." That tune, "Wah Wah," would never be a Beatles song but would wind up, appropriately, on a work entitled *All Things Must Pass.*

EVERETT

GRANGER

MIRRORPIX/EVERETT

GEORGE SAID the dissonant song "Wah Wah" was descriptive of his Beatles "headache," and its short lyric originally included the words: "You've given me a Wah Wah/So I'm thinking of you/And different things I must do." Clearly upset and perhaps embarrassed by the on-camera argument with Paul on January 6, 1969, he told his three bandmates four days later that he was quitting. "I thought, 'I'm quite capable of being happy on my own,'" he later said. "If I'm not able to be happy in this situation, I'm getting out of here." After a conciliatory meeting on January 15, George returned to the fold, but the end was nigh. The now legendary lunchtime concert on the roof of the Apple building in London, which was staged on January 30, 1969, was not a fond and romantic farewell to their fans by the Beatles (although Paul does appear in this frame to be waving goodbye), but rather an attempt to come up with some kind of climax for the film, whose working title, *Get Back*, would later be changed to *Let It Be*. Even in 1970, the Beatles kept some of the more unpleas- ant recent incidents, such as George quitting, from being included in the film. And ever since the 1980s, the movie has been generally unavailable, exist- ing only in bootlegged editions and on ancient VCR tapes. Rumored DVD reissues have been consistently blocked by the Beatles. This was not how they wished to be remembered—and certainly not how they wished to remember themselves.

LIBERATED

All things must pass, and all boys and girls must grow up to become the men and women they were meant to be. Thus with George, who found his best and most meaningful self as a solo act—if always in concert with his family, and his God.

ON THE previous spread, George and Billy Preston, are joyously in the groove together in 1974 as costars of George's band during a tour stopover in Landover, Maryland. Preston had provided keyboard support (at George's invitation) and enormous bonhomie (or at least desperately needed civility) to the Beatles' last *Let It Be* sessions as well as the rooftop concert—and therefore Preston is, in these pages, our final Fifth Beatle. At right, George is happy indeed at the center of a conclave of fellow members of the International Society for Krishna Consciousness—a.k.a. Hare Krishnas—on March 5, 1970, when they were helping him with his recordings. George was the only Beatle to adopt the Hindu faith.

HULTON-DEUTSCH/CORBIS

OPPOSITE, George sings passionately at New York City's Madison Square Garden during one of the two concerts he spearheaded on August 1, 1971, to raise money that might help the war- and cyclone-ravaged East Pakistani region known as Bangladesh. George's friend and mentor, the Indian sitarist Ravi Shankar (above), had suggested to George that perhaps there could be a small fundraiser, and George had run with the notion, phoning all his famous friends. Joining him on stage that day were, among others, Shankar, Eric Clapton, Bob Dylan (top), Billy Preston, Leon Russell and Ringo. Paul begged off, citing the absurdity of the Beatles reuniting so soon after disbanding. John was approached too, but when George insisted that Yoko not accompany him, that became a no-go. Some 40,000 people attended the shows and over 15 million dollars were ultimately raised for UNICEF's Bangladesh relief fund. Even today, sales of the terrific concert CDs and DVDs add to the coffers and good deeds of the George Harrison Fund for UNICEF, one of the charities that survive him.

AS WE SAW earlier with George and Sinatra, the times themselves provided for some unusual summit meetings, at which hairstyles and so much else contrasted humorously. (One can only imagine the conversations!) Opposite, George meets President Gerald Ford's Secretary of State Henry Kissinger in 1976; it has been said that Kissinger wasn't quite sure who George was, or why he was being asked to say hi. Right, top: George and his mates, including Ravi Shankar and the splendiferously hirsute Billy Preston, meet with President Ford at the White House on December 13, 1974, and then (bottom) our honored member of the Order of the British Empire sees what it might feel like to be an honorable member of the U.S. Cabinet. It was George who gained entrée to 1600 Pennsylvania Avenue for these funky folks, and not just because he was a Beatle. This was in the period when he was equally well known for pioneering the idea that famous folk should give back when they can, an idea that in the years ahead would inspire Live Aid's Bob Geldof and Michael Jackson's "We Are the World," and benefits by dozens of other rock stars, including George's former bandmate Paul. Geldof and McCartney are now known as Sir Bob and Sir Paul in England (well, Geldof is known that way, though being Irish his title is *technically* something other), and George certainly should have been similarly knighted in his day. Jackson, as an American, was of course ineligible, and had to settle for King of Pop.

GEORGE COULD GET darned serious about subjects such as Bangladesh or Krishna consciousness (not to mention Formula One car racing), but he could get darned silly when in the company of (and under the influence of) the likes of close friend Eric Idle. Below he performs in *Monty Python's Life of Brian*, the cult hit 1979 comedy he funded with his freshly formed HandMade Films production company. (If you put up two million pounds, you get uncredited cameos.) At left he is also under the humiliating influence of the Pythons. *Life of Brian* was a vigorously irreverent cinematic retelling of the New Testament, and was condemned as blasphemous in many quarters (it was marketed in Sweden as "the film that is so funny that it was banned in Norway"). But George was happy to be associated with it, and with Idle, whose help he had already solicited in making promotional footage in Henley-on-Thames for his 1976 album *33 1/3* (opposite: With Idle's coaxing George certainly sported some marvelous mufti). George also supported Idle's Beatles sendup *All You Need Is Cash*, which Ringo and John found very funny as well. Paul, initially upset, came around after he found out that Idle grew up in the Liverpool environs. Ringo and George even considered performing with two of Idle's "Rutles" in a supergroup based on the bands' entwined histories, but nothing came of this flight of fancy.

IN 1970, in a certainly ironic real-estate deal, the Krishna devotee bought a 34-acre, 120-room Victorian neo-gothic estate that had been a Roman Catholic school, and relocated with his wife, Pattie, from their psychedelically decorated spread in Esher to this equally eccentric estate, Friar Park, in Henley-on-Thames. Before the nuns had set up shop, Friar Park had been owned by Frank Crisp, an eminent English barrister who had been awarded a baronetcy in 1913. Crisp built sensational gardens on the grounds (George would nurture these gardens as he would those on his Hawaiian property), as well as a 20-foot-tall sandstone replica of the Matterhorn. Go figure. Many Beatles fans got their first glimpse of Friar Park when they saw the curious George-and-lawn-gnomes photograph on the cover of the *All Things Must Pass* box set, an LP collection that included "Ballad of Sir Frankie Crisp (Let it Roll)." George generally followed Crisp's policy of letting the public enjoy Friar Park's horticultural splendor until John Lennon's assassination in 1980, at which point he closed the gates.

PATTIE HARRISON and George had since broken up, and in the late summer of 1978 Olivia Arias (right, at Friar Park with George) gave birth to Dhani Harrison and shortly thereafter became George's second wife. A native of Mexico, she had met the ex-Beatle when working at A&M Records in Los Angeles. Life at Friar Park was just about as blissful as George had ever known, and he sought to make it perfect. He toiled in the gardens along with his brothers, Peter and Harry, and within the walls converted a guest suite into a state-of-the-art recording studio with 16-track equipment. (It was said to be better, overall, than the facilities at Abbey Road.) In the 1980s and '90s, George would make his music at home, oversee his movie business, venture to the stage occasionally—spurred on several occasions by his charitable impulse—and enjoy a more secluded life than Paul, certainly, and even Ringo. He had in fact become the quiet Beatle.

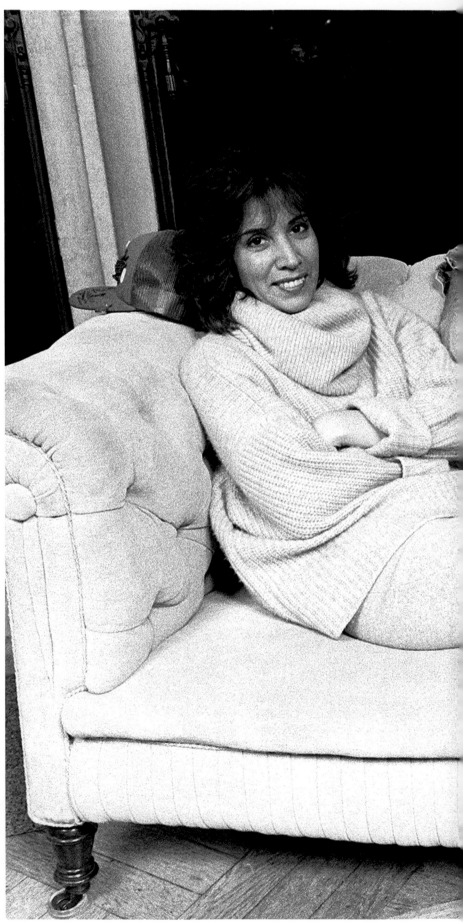

REX/EVERETT (3)

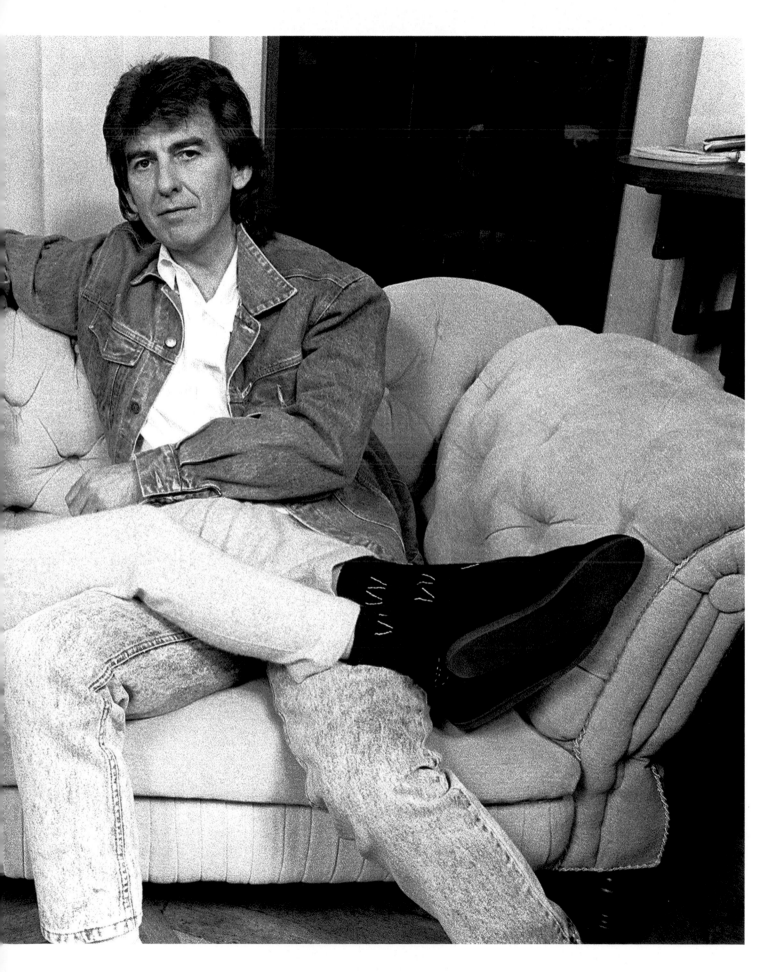

"DHA" AND "NI" are the sixth and seventh notes of the Indian music scale, but incorporated as the name of a boy raised in the Western world, they sound like "Danny." As opposed to his father and his father's old friends from Liverpool, Dhani was raised in extraordinary privilege at Friar Park, went to the best schools, was able to put his smarts on display and ultimately graduate from the Ivy League's Brown University, which earlier had nurtured John F. Kennedy Jr. and today is the academic home of Dhani's countrywoman Emma Watson, of *Harry Potter* fame. He was close to his dad, and loved being taken by him to Grand Prix car races. Dhani hadn't planned to become a professional musician, but these things happen (right, delighted to be layering guitars with his father in 1992 at London's Royal Albert Hall during a benefit concert for the Natural Law Party). When George left behind an incomplete album, *Brainwashed*, upon his death in November 2001, Dhani helped finish it. A few years later, he started his own band, and recently he has teamed with Ben Harper and Joseph Arthur in Fistful of Mercy, a latter-day so-called supergroup that he says reminds him, warmly, of his father's participation in the Traveling Wilburys. In listening to the lovely harmonies in Fistful of Mercy music, one word, long in the lexicon, comes immediately to mind: *Beatlesque*.

LINDA MCCARTNEY

ARENAPLEX/EVERETT

IT WAS BUSINESS that brought Paul, George and Ringo together at Friar Park in earliest summer of 1994 and again in '95 at Paul's farm (above). The plan was that they were going to reminisce and perhaps even record Beatles songs, including "Let It Be," for use in *The Beatles Anthology* project. But the mood quickly turned more human than businesslike, as John's absence was palpable. During a private, hours-long talk among the three at Friar Park, George in particular said that they simply shouldn't do it. Eventually, his opinion held sway. The rest of the day proved to be great good fun, as they sang the oldest tunes—"Raunchy," "Ain't She Sweet," "Blue Moon of Kentucky"—never pretending to be the Beatles, but just three good, longtime friends. Years earlier, as we know, Paul and John hadn't shown up for George's Bangladesh concerts, but in 2002, when Olivia Harrison and Eric Clapton organized the Concert for George in London on the anniversary of her husband's death, of course Paul and Ringo were there—along with Billy Preston, Ravi Shankar, Tom Petty, all of them. Dhani played that night at Royal Albert Hall (opposite)—precisely a decade after he had weaved guitar lines with his father on the same stage—and was thereby introduced to the global music audience. Paul, who had met young George when they were schoolboys all those years ago in Liverpool on the bus driven by Mr. Harrison, observed poignantly at one point: "Olivia said that with Dhani up on stage, it looks like George stayed young and we all got old." George, with all he believed about life and life's progression, would have gotten a huge kick out of that. And who knows? Maybe, looking down, he did.

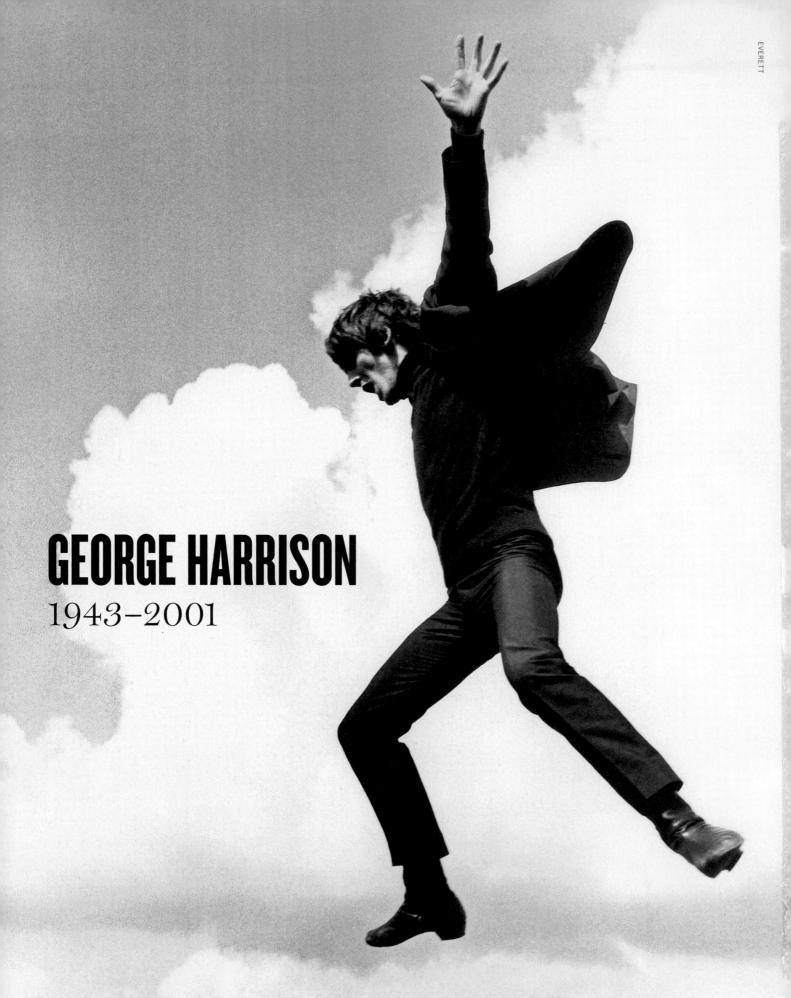

GEORGE HARRISON
1943–2001